an identity polyptych

an id
poly

TAMECA L COLEMAN

entity
ptych

THE ELEPHANTS

22 23 24 5 4 3 2

Distributed by Small Press Distribution, Inc.

The Elephants Ltd.
theelephants.net

ISBN 978-1-988979-44-1 print

Cover design by Aimee Harrison

Typeset in Spectral (Production Type)
and Juana (Latinotype) by Aimee Harrison

Author Photo by Tameca L Coleman

contents

I do not know when reconciliation comes

"I thought there was a thing called forgiveness, and if you don't
want to forgive and if you don't pray for that person, it never be right."

An activist writes: "Reconciliation is dead,"
the captioned photograph of a beautiful Native woman
shouting, a red hand painted over her mouth.

I am reminded of a man who is dead now
and who admitted to me
the rape on his record

before asking me
to stand between him and community,
some of whom knew, some who didn't, to soften, I imagine the
knowledge of his past

and I asked a friend who had been gang-
raped if they thought a rapist could be rehabilitated.

and I remembered the traumas in the bodies of those I worked for,
and wondered what kind of person I would be if I said yes.

My mother's neck still shakes, and the only power she has these
days is in safeguarding her broken body.

I had a friend who had smooshy feelings for someone, and for
his warmth another man ripped his insides, and left him, asking if he
liked that.

He had no one, so though he didn't like that, he accepted the only security he thought could be found, and then the rest of them, too, had their turns. This is the price he paid for a home, he told me, and he thought that maybe he deserved it, the taking and tearing of his insides. He went back again and again.

A lover once said, "Your body is not always yours. Let me have it."

A lover once said, "You are being preserved for me, and I will find you. Do you like to be raped?"

A lover once told me that I better not dare claim anything other than love, my placement in his bed secured by the rifle within arm's reach.

A lover once told me about the "sanctuary" found where two men made all the children they saved trade sexual favors. She is nostalgic about this house, and speaks the magic of floor beds and shared scarcities. This world was somehow better than what she had before, and she sometimes wonders where those men have gone, and she sometimes craves small dusty spaces and booze and shared bread that's already turning.

Someone somewhere will no longer catcall a woman and yell into her back that he's talking to her because of the scream that scraped scars up my throat and out of my mouth.

Someone somewhere has eight long scars down his back for trying to force me to take a "picture" to remember him by.

Someone somewhere carries my mother's stab wound.

I do not know when reconciliation comes.

When you said, "You know, there's two sides to every story. I guess your Mom did what she did and I just went off."

> I thought about how I hate violence,
> and I thought about how we're facing violence all the time,
> the perpetrators of the wounds we carry getting off
> scott-free with the language of their gods in tow,
> beating us over our heads once again
> with demands for forgiveness
> songs we do not owe.

my Blackness is
a constant question

They Were Made For Us

I remember this shopkeeper
as the Oakland Sentinel.

His arms
cross over his chest,
his face gruff, tone condemning:

"What do *you* want with those cowries?"

He is protecting the stock. He is protecting it from me.

I look to my friend and she says nothing.
We are pinned in the pause, hitches
in the summer heat. This man
waits for my answer.
He waits.

I want to make a necklace. Mine is broken, see?

The braid holds a row of mouths
but the line that holds them is broken,
the knot that connects the circle,
unloosed.

Outside, people are moving towards a dream.
I love this Oakland—a bustle where a whole neighborhood
remakes itself in its own image against the world around it —
But, this is also a world where buildings are left to rot
in wait of big pockets that will soon redevelop all the lots.

I think: Encroachment.
I think: I am a tourist here.
I think: I cannot possibly know.

I tell the sentinel, "Because they are the mouths of the Orishas."
I want him to see I know they are powerful.
I want him to see I know they are the mouths
from which everything is born.

His eyes have me in lock.
I think: I am not a thief.

Asante, my friend—
Her voice made of bells and kid-laughter
shouts, "Because they were made for us!"

The sentinel looks towards her
and softens. Her head is wrapped.
She wears bead and bone.

He motions permission towards the bins,
and I turn to them. At last!
But the cowries,
all of them,
are broken

at the teeth.

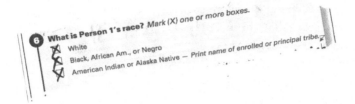

Am I Black?

I put my hand to the drum,
straddled the woodburned neck,
pounded into the skin whose spine
ran down the center. I wrote my own
message under the rim,
cut and wetted the drumhead,
tightened and tuned the drum.

I wore cowries around my neck
stared into their mouths
and palmed them, ran my fingers
down their teeth.

I tied them on with bells
and danced the Damballa
in my living room. I danced
to CD drummers and rain forest people's
singing. I danced stories
about moving forward even when the wind
pushes you back. Was it a parable
from my ancestors?
I do not know. I do not
know them.

I watched the dances
at an opening ceremony for Adefua. I danced
at dancehall night in Oakland. I tried
to do the Electric Slide
at a summer cookout. I listened
to the elders speak. I
sang songs to Kori, I
tried to beckon Chango.

I made my voice ring like the Ba-Benzélé.
I layered my voice like the Ba-Benzélé.
I looped rhythms to emulate them.
I know what Uhuru means.
Uhuru Uhuru Laiye Freedom!
I have sung that freedom song
from a stage in Idaho.

And I have been in the church
even if I am not of it. I sang "He 'rose.
He 'rose. He 'rose from the dead."
I watched women talk in tongues there.
I ate their home cooking after the service.
They pinched my cheeks and called me
Beautiful.

They asked me whose daughter
I was. I do not know whose
daughter I am.

A friend of mine says that to call myself brown in any context is a choice, and a privilege that undercuts this question of Blackness. [I am Black].

On the bus, a woman looks straight at me, and says: You know you Black, right? I tentatively nod. She says: I'm just making sure, because sometimes y'all don't know you Black. [I am Black].

In Oakland, a sweet Black man asks: Who that big pretty brown girl is? We play slap-'em-on-the-table dominoes. I wish I was staying. [I am Black.]

... And so often brown or POC seems so much more right or safer, because how many times have I been told I'm not really Black, or I'm not Black enough? [I am Black].

... And so often brown or POC seems so much more right or safer, because how many times have I seen privilege denied when you are anything more than quiet and ambiguous? [I am Black].

A Black girlfriend reminds: "If I'm doing it, Black people do it." [I am Black. I am Black. I am Black].

"For all practical purposes, 'race' is not so much a biological phenomenon as a social myth. The myth of 'race' has created an enormous amount of human and social damage. In recent years it has taken a heavy toll in human lives and caused untold suffering. It still prevents the normal development of millions of human beings and deprives civilization of the effective co-operation of productive minds. The biological differences between ethnic groups should be disregarded from the standpoint of social acceptance and social action. The unity of mankind from both the biological and social viewpoints is the main thing. To recognize this and to act accordingly is the first requirement of modern man."

It never matters until I leave the house.

"When I walk out that door, no one cares about my history, or my culture. They don't care about who I am, or what I do, or what I know. When I walk out that door, they don't see me, they see a black man, and that is all I am to them. Remember that." Quote from Al Jazeera, "Race in the US: What if your identity was a lie?" by John Metta.

"When you call yourself an Indian or a Muslim or a Christian or a European, or anything else, you are being violent. Do you see why it is violent? Because you are separating yourself from the rest of mankind. When you separate yourself by belief, by nationality, by tradition, it breeds violence. So a man who is seeking to understand violence does not belong to any country, to any religion, to any political party or partial system; he is concerned with the total understanding of mankind."

It became apparent, my privilege, when out of my mouth came the following words: "I couldn't believe that she was running away from *me*."

She was one of the new neighborhood people, young, white and affluent enough to afford one of the brand-new popup pressboard luxury homes that had replaced the old working class 'hood.

I had two bags of groceries in each hand, and she was looking over both shoulders, jangling her keys, and quickening her pace. I mean, what *did* she think I was going to do? Ask her to help me carry my groceries?

Now I have fantasies of running across the street every time I see her brand of white person. In the fantasy I frantically yell over my shoulders, "Leave me alone! I've done nothing to you! Please! Do not hurt me!" And then, arms flailing, I keep running.

Inside, Outside, the Ocean

1.

Outside of you is a great emptiness:

They push around their dirt and call themselves
holy.

      They ignore their silt.
      Their silt is in you.
      There is silt in you.

You are overly aware of your dirt.
In freshwater, you sit.
In salt, you muddle.

      They took
      the broom and pushed you over the edge.

The dirt
is an anchor

      heavier
      than water, you first float,
      then sink,

all around you is a caressing darkness.
the silt
an undulation
in the belly. The silt
becomes a head turning,
limbs waving.

The dirt is a mirror
that makes of the body
an elegance

before the body becomes the sea.

In one view it is a beckoning dance;
in another, a painful writhing.

2.

They've spit their own myths with their silt over the edge.

3.

You must transcend your state through telepathy.
Nobody knows you, even if you are a god's daughter.

4.

You are too far from the root.
They will have to pull you up
and decide what you are.

                Most likely, a haunt they do not want to remember.
Or maybe, confessor. They want you to be the voice of all that forgives them.
Or maybe something meant only to fulfill their hunger, the silt
again transferred. A full circle met. You are a fish with a woman's face.
They will throw the bones and the eyes back over the edge.

5.

Inside of you is a great emptiness:

There is a memory thick as your pumping blood.
The memory was once a boat
whose drops in the ocean tick along the clock face,
a ball and chain secured at a succession of ankles,
reversed hangmen, the arms reaching up towards a diminutional sun.

6.

You are a muddling of
silt and sadness, a series
of question marks reaching toward
sunlight, curved in and anchored
to the line of earth that defines you,
the period after a well-formed sentence,
the anchor of an opening arch.

7.

Inside of you is a great expanse:

You are the ocean. Nobody even knows.
You are an ocean, and the ships and fish keep passing.
You are an ocean, the great salt water bridge, the great corroder.
You are that powerful. You are the ocean's daughter.
Those who threw you here and did not know dare not
stay long lest their boats fail,
lest they sink, lest the water gods turn them into the sea.

8.

Outside of you is a great expanse:

You are the awkward pause in a howistheweather conversation,
not even a storm cloud, though you might mention it.

What are you? Not even a bird's wing because
birdsofafeather. You wish you knew how it would feel to be free.
Like a bird in the sky. How sweet that would be! But is not a bird
anchored to its flock? The arcs and dots are echomarks
flying out of your mouth.

Damballa

Old saying says,
"If you can walk you can ..."

    With the blinds drawn tight and sun on the pane, I dance.

Neighbors can't see the outline of limb's shadows
waving
    and signing
    behind the shades.

I sway,
Stamp to my CD drummers.

    I am sweat and flush and labored breath,
    some priestess of snakes
    guiding a procession
    of silk
    clad ladies
    across
    a snake charmed floor.

Our arms
slither like waxed and red scales.

    We are solitarians
crossing trees for coils
of rest.

    Fingers flicker like tongues
    lapping onto soft palettes.

We dance,
feel drumbeats spiral up through thighs, bellies, chests, arms.

We dance
until hoods raised, backs swayed, hips and spines thrive.

We dance
until we've forgotten the meaning of the song,
and it doesn't matter if we know all the steps.

A Shape Story

disturbing story

by Tameca Coleman

1

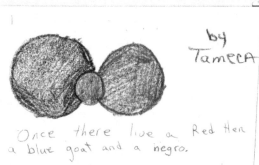

by Tameca

Once there live a Red Hen a blue goat and a negro.

2

Then one day the blue goat went to get some stew.

Then the negro went away and the blue goat came back.

Then afterwards the Red hen followed the negro and left the blue goat all alone.

Then __Mean__ Indians came and serounded the poor blue goat.

Then the hen and the negro came back and scared the Indians away

But the Indian came back and the made them go back to their village.

THE END

"The work is never ending. The revolution that must take place is inside us.

"Revolution is not a one-time event. It is becoming always vigilant for the smallest opportunity to make a genuine change in established, outgrown responses; for instance, it is learning to address each other's difference with respect."

Audre Lorde, *Sister Outsider.*

You can't just read your way out of racism. And yet reading with that aim is a powerful and viable first step. And how strange when you pair that against a Black man and his partner creating a space for communing and intervention, full of informative and empowering books meant for the communities they come from, for the communities whose safe spaces are disappearing, for the communities who are being colonized and owned all over again.

The young man who comes to speak to us has grit in his teeth when he says "white liberals." They are the ones who have money and they are happy to spend it here. Spending their money here makes them feel that they are doing something. They do not realize that even here, they are co-opting intent. They do not realize that even here, in their earnest desire to understand, they harm.

am i an ally?

you can't read yourself
out of racism

but stacks of books line the desks
                and tables,
        the bedside dressers,

            they line
                the insides of my bags.

            i take notes and carry
            the weight of them.
            i underline
            and highlight. read   with yearning.
            the more i read, the more i know
                    i know

        nothing

                    i bend over the tables, my shoulders
                              curving over my heart, eyes
                                   strain and water,
                    my chest heaves.
each book
is a silent soldier
          armed to the edge of the pages'
slicing corners   see
          see
                    see
how
my spine compresses.

see how
my fingers
bleed.

My Black

1.

is an actual infinity.

I am the transformative dark.

In the night, there are stars:
cubed and repeating,
fashioning after a multitude.

These eyes are portals squared.

2.

is the safe bet.

and the one drop rule
still applies.

I tell them
I am not convenient.
They tell me
they need
more Black friends.

3.

is a judgement against me.

The kids on the bus called me
one name after another.
This time, "Zebra."

I spent the whole next night
attempting to create a good comeback. I lay
in my bed long past bedtime, smiling when at last I had it.
In the morning on the way to school,
I asked: Where are the stripes?
They said: Melted in.

The class bully decided he could get away with it.
He said: You're nothing but a nigger.
I told him that nigger
was a river
in Africa.
He said: No.
It's Niger,
Stupid.

That night I consulted
the dust caked encyclopedias on our bookshelves.
Niger has one g. Nigger has two.

4.

is half magic

        between   things

limbo tweenie

        dusk and twilight

a steam between the windows

frost on the glass
froth on the glasshouse
half-caste magistrate.

I am between

a steamroller and the windpipes,
a half-day
frown on the glaze.

I am a half-life magnet
steel between windshields.
Fruitcake on the glen

between half-notes
a steelworker
a halfpenny
between thirsts
a steeple between wings,
half-sister magic deathflowers in her hair
crooning crooning still
strange fruit hanging
      on the tree.

I am between thistles

a steeplechase

halftone magpie
inside two thoraxes

a heifer between winks
fuddy-duddy on the glimpse.

half-wit
between thorns,
        a pedestrian
        that glistens
and burns.

I am between thoughts
a line inside the shoulder
a fugitive between thrashes

a stenographer without tools
fulminating against the globe.

5.

makes one man on the phone
tell me my name is a Black girl's name.
This midwestern schoolgirl speak—
He wants to know why I have a Black girl's name.
"Yes," I say. "I am part that."
And, "what is the reason for your call?"
He still wants to know why I have a Black girl's name.

6.

is [?]: ?

They think I am approachable because I render myself nondescript.
My clothes are utilitarian, mostly black, no labels facing.
I have cut my hair. No one touches it anymore
and they've stopped asking me what I am.

7.

is blood.

Should I cut out my mother
burning red in the sun?

Toothpick Shortly After 9/11

I stand in line, waiting my turn to purchase a couple of money orders. A man waiting at the counter wears a laundered baseball cap that conforms perfectly to his head. He turns around to face me, sizes me up and down a peg or two. He twists his toothpick a few times, takes it out, looks at the end of it before proceeding to dig between a new set of teeth. He lets the toothpick set in his mouth so he can move it around with his tongue and chew on it some.

"Where you from?" he asks. His head moves a click upwards as he does.

I pause. I already know what he means, and I tell him I am probably more American than our president. Maybe even more than he is.

"You don't say. How's that?"

I was born in Texas on an airforce base that doesn't exist anymore.

The man chuckles and mutters, "Texas huh?" He looks down, considering. He moves the toothpick to the other side of his mouth.

The cashier comes back with the manager. The man doesn't look at me again. He leaves, his back towards me the whole time. My skin burns.

"Mardket Woooomon! Mardket Woooomon! Sailing all 'er goodz at Kings-tohn Mahrdkeht! Mardket Woooomon! Whoooooah! Mardket Woooomon!"

Mr. V, our substitute choral director motions for the class to stop singing. He tells us how thin our sound is. We sound like a bunch of white people, he tells us. He points to me and says, "Sing it like they do in Africa."

My brother and I are the only two brown people in this class. I often joke that we are half magic. One time I walked in late and saw our choir teacher showing the class how to snap on beats two and four instead of on one and three in a four-beat bar. She explained how getting the feel of swing was like following an egg's motion as it rolled down a hill.

I remember thinking, "Wow. So, this really happens." I watched for a while before stepping back to my seat and tried not to giggle. Some of my classmates were getting it, some of them weren't, all of them were trying so hard.

I thought of that opening scene on the porch in "The Jerk," where Steve Martin's character, who was "born a poor Black child," can't find the beat, hard as he tries. And a later scene where he starts snapping and tapping to a swing song on the radio. He thinks he has found "the rhythm" (well, he's found some kind of rhythm) and he snaps and clicks his feet to-gether on beats one and three of a four beat bar.

Duke Ellington used to teach folks how to snap on the right beat. He'd exaggerate his snap to emulate the pulse of the swing, pulling the poised snap upwards on one and letting the whole hand drop to snap on two. It was a conductor's move. And he had a lecture to go along with it: "of course one never snaps one's fingers *on* the beat. It's considered aggressive. You don't push it, you just let it fall." Then he'd look across the audience and let them know what cool sounded like. "And if you would like to be conservatively hip...tilt the earlobe," "and if you're cooler than that, then of course, you tilt the left earlobe on the beat and snap the finger on the afterbeat. And then you really don't care. And so....one can become as cool as one wishes to be."

I'm not sure if I'm cool or not (you know, I'm half magic), even if I can snap and tap. But, I don't know a dingdang about Africa. I did see *The Power of One*, and I listened to the official soundtrack for a week.

I think about the deep, open timbre of the African voices singing in that film and try to emulate it. Mr. V is encouraging and asks me to do it again. He wants me to give it more umph. I sing my best Mardket Woooomon, only louder this time. Mr. V tells me it's better but I should give it one more go. I take a deep breath to start, trying not to make a face. I sing so much in my mouth my chest and teeth tingle.

Mr. V is satisfied, and tells everyone in the room to do it like that.

My Blackness is a Constant Question

When Curtis Mayfield sings, "High yellow girl, can't you tell / you're just the surface of our dark deep well? / If your mind could really see / you'd know your color the same as me."

When Toni Morrison observes that "Now people choose their identities. Now people choose to be Black. They used to be *born* Black. That's not true anymore. You can be Black genetically and choose not to be. You can change your mind or your eyes, change anything. It's just a mindset."

Rachel Dolezal. Martina Big. Jessica Krug. Blackfishers on Instagram. Those of us who can pass as white. Those of us who can be racially ambiguous.

In Oakland, walking through a beautiful, old money neighborhood with established trees, I say that I would love to live in a place like that. My friend turns to say, "and what? Forget about *our* people?"

My classmates get mad at Ourika for not siding more with "her people" and I try not to speak, but I feel everyone waiting for me to say something because they think I will agree. I am the only brown person in class. Ourika hadn't grown up in the communities in question. Neither had I.

Every time I was told I wasn't Black enough to talk about Blackness because I talked like white people and didn't grow up in the right neighborhoods.

"B-L-A-C-K, N-U-S-S. B-L-A-C-K, N-U-S-S. B-L-A-C-K, N-U-S-S. B-L-A-C-K, Black is okay!"

That time I walked up to the cash register at REI and the cashier looked me up and down and said my mother must be proud because I was so polite and because I talked so well.

No one ever believes there are Black people in Idaho.

That one time I went to see this singer I loved and she slapped me on my backside and asked, "How'd you get an ass like that?!"

That time I won a songwriting contest in junior high school for MLK, sang it on the capitol steps, and was asked by Reverend A's children, "What are you doing with a voice like that?"

That moment when this man stood up after Peggy Macintosh's "White Privilege: Unpacking the Invisible Backpack" assembly and said, "you all have to remember that the one drop rule still applies. It is still the law!" and I turned around so he wouldn't see my face.

That moment in *Black-ish* when Dre tells Bow she's not really Black.

My initial excitement over Jean Toomer's writings about mixed-race peoples, and realizing race never matters until I open the door, and that Toomer stopped writing and became a recluse.

I dated a man from the French Congo. I dated a man who was mixed like me. I dated a Black man who laughed and told me those two men weren't real Black men.

You probably like those light skinned boys.
"You cannot possibly know what I like."

I am in grade school. The survey asks me what I am. I check Black, White, American Indian or Alaskan Native, and Other.

Frank Romero and Gitz Crazyboy tell me that I am all of those things, and should be all of those things in the world. What other way is there to be?

When #BlackLivesMatter was fresh, so many of the people I knew who also had no or few other Black friends rushed to tell me that they were my allies, that they would fight for me so that the emotional labor wasn't laid on my shoulders, and then I realized, while it's nice to be recognized as Black, *I* needed more Black friends.

I write to the president of my school's Black Student Alliance. I ask: How do I learn what it means to be Black? No answer.

That palpable silence after a light-skinned slam poet apologizes for three minutes for being half.

"Aren't you a little dark to be in this neighborhood?" This is what they say to my brothers. They lick their lips at me.

When Janelle Monae stepped onto the scene.

When Logic stepped onto the scene.

On the eve of my eighteenth birthday, I cut off my long hair. It was so long people used to ask me how I went to the bathroom. In grade school, they used to pretend my two pony tails were double dutch ropes. Mom angrily said I cut my hair to look like the white girls at school. I just wanted the white girls to leave my hair alone.

When I saw "Good and Bad Hair" in *School Daze* for the first time.

My Mother told me how heartbroken she was because she thought she had brought us up in such a way that race wouldn't matter. Now I am writing about racism.

When my stepDad said all I have to do is take care of A-1 Number One and be Black and be Proud.

Every time I heard James Brown shout, "Say it loud!" and wondered if I had the right.

Every time I was accused of being self-hating Black.

When Rebecca Walker warns that "if we remain mesmerized by the idea of ourselves as eternally broken, we all but guarantee the loss of our lives as fully functional, whole human beings."

That moment I said, "Do I look Black to you?" and my mother about jumped out of her seat to slap some sense into me and I said, "but my friends think it's funny."

A Cat Named Nigger

At fifteen, I was good with being paid under the table. That's why I was watching this worn, wrinkled woman tug on a third long cigarette as she interviewed me.

The woman needed someone to housesit a couple of nights. She seemed to like me. I didn't have classes till Monday, and I could get away from Mom's house as much as I wanted to. The woman said she had a cat. I liked cats.

I don't remember what we talked about. I only remember that she had stacks and stacks of yellowed Harlequin Romances on a table. I remember she wore short shorts and a tank top that day, pastel. She was thin, her skin was thin, her fingernails were painted and her hair was cropped short. She lit another cigarette.

A cat trill interrupted us. I turned to see it. It was black but for its eyes and whiskers. It looked like a stray.

"Come here, Nigger," the woman said, crouching down as she clicked her tongue and wiggled her fingers. Then she paused, sat up abruptly, and then looked at me with a strain on her face. I held my breath. The cat ignored the woman as it passed, arching its back away from my hand.

"Oh, that's the cat's name," the woman said, smashing the end of her cigarette into an already full ashtray. "I hope that wasn't offensive." She waited for me to answer.

I shrugged to put the woman at ease, and I housesat for her anyway.

Am I Black?

childhood

We look happy here

What would have happened if I had the stupid courage to wade through corn fields to the abandoned house that called to me from a few acres away? I used to sit quietly rocking on the swingset, feet digging a hole in the clay dirt, staring across to it. I wanted to see its insides, and live without the sway of adults.

I stood tall in our yard, poised to sprint, daring myself to slam my body into the drying corn, against green and amber stalks, but something kept me from it. Maybe it was the light in our yard, dim enough already for cricket chirps and the fat croaks of frogs. Maybe it was the bats swooping, clipping at my hair as the mosquitoes bit and the fireflies began to glint in the woods.

Mom reminded about the threat of woodland animals: rabid dogs, snakes, muskrats. She taught the possibility of innumerable wounds— a claw slash, a poisoned bite, teeth gnawing straight to the arm and leg bones.

Even the deer could be dangerous. I had a dream that they stared at me through bare skulls. I was afraid of the hardness of their antlers and hooves.

One day Mom and Dad decided we would go to it. They'd heard abandoned houses held treasures. Three kids were extra hands robbing the place. At least that's how I remember it. I remember us as thieves.

We drove up the brambled dirt path and stopped for blackberries— wild, tart, and warm with their summer heat. We were a family in those moments.

When we got to the house, we pushed through the rickety screen and pried open the door. We saw a dirty boxspring and mattress in the front room amid a jumble of everything that once served as a home resting in dust and sharp slants of sunlight.

It looked as though it could be saved— a little tending, a little paint, a little TLC, a little breath, my coloring books, my favorite toys, my own life.

I considered the mattress and wondered how to fend against fleas and bedbugs. I took inventory: tossed-aside chairs, dusty tables, cabinets. I don't remember pictures on the walls but there were broken dishes in the sink, broken windows with torn curtains, bric-a-brac. There was barely a toe path through the broken furniture and debris.

Official documents showed through an opening in the mattress. I asked Mom if we should take them, remembering old Westerns where homeowners hid banknotes and leases in the bed. I tried to decipher a wealth from those pages, but Mom said they weren't worth anything.

I watched her tread carefully as she surveyed the downstairs. She turned in slow circles. Then, she and Dad tried to move a dresser. It wouldn't budge. "We have a lot of furniture anyway," Mom said.

Mom shrilled that something was moving. I think Dad talked her out of her fear. It was a mouse. Even our home had vermin in the walls. It was just a part of living by fields.

I looked up and saw the stairs' uncertain fixtures. I was sure I was light enough to bound over the broken boards. I pointed up, asked if we could look. Mom tentatively tried the first few steps and shook her head.

We took furniture, maybe other things. My memory is fuzzy. Mom doesn't remember. My father won't say.

In a later trip, a gift for me: an antique vanity with three mirrors. It was placed near the foot of my bed—a piece of furniture that required the hands of not only my father, but some of my uncles, maybe some of their friends. I remember my father looking for a response, as if the vanity was all the love in the world.

I would rarely walk in front of it and at night I turned the mirror leaves in. I'd seen shadows move across the surface and around the foot of my bed. It was a trick of the eyes, a product of my guilty conscience, Mom said.

I would wrap myself into the bedding, make sure it covered my head, that my feet were tucked. I'd hide there, invisible, keep the cool of the night from creeping in. I'd sleep, or pretend to, until soft slants of sunlight dissolved the dark and I could open the three mirrors again.

We Chucked Rocks at the Woodland Haunts

We were tempted by the woods' mysteries and the abandoned shacks up the road, artifacts of the neighboring families who used to live there among the weeds. But, we were forbidden to explore those places. We were restricted to the confines of our mother's yard: half an acre of beat up grass surrounded by the woods, the fields, and a country dirt road.

Mom warned about the many dangers waiting poised in the long grasses around the shacks. She told us the shacks were rickety, sure to collapse on top of curious children. We'd have to go to the edge of the woods to break off a green switch if we disobeyed, and none of us wanted that.

Summers were heavy, green and wood musk, punctuated by the dust of passing cars and combines. The heat pushed down on us, and we were sticky with its weight. We sprayed each other with the hose until the horse flies caught on that we were children with skin soaked and tender. Then we'd swat and run squealing around the yard.

We knew that folks from the shacks were closer to the mysteries of the woods that we wanted to know for ourselves. My brother and I could only watch the woods from the safety of our mother's yard. We crept down towards the road, getting as close to the cooled tree shadows and the line of summer corn.

We knew that the children who lived in the roadside shacks ducked in and out of the woods to hide from each other and to see what they could find. They made games in the cornfields, their dogs trailing behind and barking, and they popped in and out of tree shadows, unafraid. The bats and the fireflies, the muskrat we heard the neighbors ate sometimes, the field mice, mosquitoes, tree snakes and the wild blackberries that grew alongside the road were in their blood.

Their parents let them chase frogs and feral cats back into the trees with whooshing sticks and rowdy yells. They could even take their toys with them to play. We had to leave our toys inside. We could only catch whatever creatures left the woods and landed in our yard, but only if Mom didn't catch us. She said wood creatures were dirty and could make us sick.

It was strange when the families left. They took their children and their music but the voices of dogs left behind haunted the woods. We heard our mother talk about the dogs. They chased the deer in and out of the woods. They chased the bats, and ate whatever they could find. They chased mice and flies and sniffed at trees and holes in the earth. I wondered if they ever feasted on a doe or a buck. I wondered what they thought of little children. Mom said they were probably rabid now.

My brother and I saw them one afternoon; the pack of wild dogs congregated at the head of our driveway, their presence emphasized by a white Great Dane. The dogs stood there and stared.

We were children with skin soaked and tender. We could not see whether the dogs' mouths frothed.

I was the big sister. I knew that it was not wise to run. I knew that we would have to run if the dogs started rushing towards us. I reached for driveway stones, chucked them in the direction of the dogs. The dogs just stared and stared.

I crouched for more stones, screamed through the heaviness in my chest at the pack. I hurled rocks so hard I could feel pain in my arm sockets and elbows. I could not throw the rocks far enough. All of them landed with a dull clack. The dogs did not budge.

My brother started throwing stones then. He was to the right and a little behind me. I could hear him begin to scream at the dogs. Our voices together became hopeless cacophony. We screamed a burn into our throats. We kept throwing stones, and the dogs kept blankly staring back.

We kept throwing rocks. We kept throwing them until the white Great Dane turned its head towards the pack, barked one time, and then trotted back into the woods. The pack of dogs followed.

My brother and I looked at one another. We stood in the driveway for what seemed a long time. We let the rocks in our hands fall back into the driveway. The dogs did not return.

The story of my name

My name is a gimmick
my mother gave me.

[No,
it's the message.

I went to school with a girl who called herself Timika, but that was her middle name. We'd see each other in the halls during passing periods and point at each other, yelling TAMEEKAH! We'd laugh before going on with our day and sometimes give each other a high five as we passed each other. That was the extent of our friendship. Timika was new, about half of the school year in. We didn't share any classes, and I kept meaning to get to know her more. Once she told me she was named after her father, hence the spelling. I liked the way Timika spelled her name.

One morning, there was an announcement over the intercom. Timika and her mother were killed in a bad accident. I was so sad, and a lot of my friends thought it was me. I hated that the energy of the hugs my classmates gave me took away from the girl who had just died, her mother fallen asleep at the wheel.

*

At high school graduation, when the principal called Tahmehka Lee Coleman, I did not budge from the front of the line. I held my breath and ground my dress shoes into the gymnasium floor.

The principal looked towards me expectantly, tilted his head a little against the crowd and pursed his lips. He knocked his head back like it was on a tiny spring, and his eyebrows furrowed an expression of heyareyoucoming. Then he said that name again.

I pressed my weight into my toes and made the graduation robe sway (the tassel on the cap too), but I did not step forward. The principal said the name once or twice again with an urgent look on his face. I still did not approach.

He had told us at practice graduation that if someone mispronounced our names on the graduation stage, we should wait until that name was corrected. This was a reiteration of one of the things that my mother always taught: "Make sure they get your name right."

I saw numerous classmates move forward despite the pronunciation of their names. My heart sank each time. I wanted to grab their shoulders and tell them to wait.

I decided I would keep standing there until my name was pronounced correctly, despite the shifting of our families and friends in the audience, despite the racket of my heartpatter, despite the look on the principal's face, despite the tingling in my toes, despite the person behind me who kept telling me it was my turn as they put their hand to my back to nudge me forward. No. I was going to stand there and wait. Tahmehka. Who was that?

I looked up, and communicated my own expression: a scrunched-up combination of "I'm sorry," and "Surely you remember how to pronounce my name." The principal had announced my name correctly over the intercom numerous times. How could he get it wrong now? I tilted my chin into an uncomfortable shrug and waited, trying not to tap my feet.

The principal limply held the papers full of names. He held himself up against the podium with his elbows in an exasperated stance. There were hundreds of names still to call.

Out of the stalled air, friends began shouting my name. "It's Tameca! It's Tameca! It's Tameca!" they said. I smiled to myself and breathed deep.

The principal motioned for me to come forward again. I waited. The room was a prolonged pause. Finally, he said it: "Tameca Lee Coleman." I quickwalked towards the podium. I looked directly at the principal and nodded, reached for his outstretched hand, shook it and accepted my diploma.

I heard the room wake up with cheers and clapping. I kept my head down and took my seat, trying to remember to keep breathing. I listened as the names rolled by with a certain clip, the following applause. I stared into the lap of my silver graduation gown until I could breathe easily again and brought my eyes up to watch and clap as the blood came back to my toes.

*

People ask me all the time if my name means anything special. I found Tamiko during a junior high school project where we had to figure out the origins of our names. I learned that Tamiko is Japanese and means "child of the people," which sounds nice. I found an ad for a porcelain doll in a National *Geographic* whose name was Tamika. The ad said Tamika meant "palm tree;" I was skeptical. In tourist shops I scoured the racks of name keychains and magnets. I saw Tammy and Tamara. By the way, don't ever call me that.

I found my name on one of those name sites. The site said that Tameca is Afro-Asiatic and has no relation to the Japanese name Tamika/o. The site doesn't know which part of Africa the name comes from. It could be from any central African state. The name might mean "sweet" or "measure," and came to the United States sometime in the seventies. That's about all anyone knows.

I was told that my name kind of sounds like Damika, which is another name that appeared in the mid-seventies and does not have a definite origin or meaning. I once knew a girl named Danica. I think someone from India told me they'd met a couple of girls named Damaka which sounds awfully close to the Urdu word for "bang or blast." I'm not sure why I know that. For some reason when I introduce myself half the people who hear me think I've said Dumeka or Sumika or ... Schumeeka (?). One person thought they heard "puta," but to be fair I don't think they knew the Spanish, and I was turning away from them when I'd said my name. Often in emails I see Tamara, and am frustrated every time..

Generally, people quickchange the subject when I try to say any of this. My explanation is too long. I'm always a little sad that they don't even crack a smile when I say that I've heard my name in a bunch of rap songs.

*

My mother used to babysit this little girl named Tameca. She loved the little girl. She loved the name. That's why she said that if she had a little girl, she would name her the same.

That's all I knew about that story for a long while, and I never thought to ask more about the little girl, not until I was over forty. When I first heard the story, I wanted to change my name.

Mom babysat for the couple next door, but they didn't seem to like her much. One night the husband came home, and looked at his wife, and cried out, "What the hell is this white bitch doing in my house?" The wife chuckled and said some things in response.

My mother went up to the man and put her palms to his cheeks, looked him straight in the eyes, and said, "Don't worry. I'll be back." She picked up her things and left to go home for the night.

Mom said things were easier after that. She got to babysit this kid she liked, the couple paid her to do it, and the man was nice to her, even respectful. Mom noticed that sometimes the wife had marks on her face from a beating. The wife used to talk shit but she stopped talking shit.

*

"Good morning, namesakes," writes the administrator for a Facebook group called Club Tamika. Her name is Tamika. She has scouted all the Tamikas, Timekas, Tamikos, Tammikkias, Temekas, Tameshias, Tammikkias, Tamiquas, Tameckas, Tahmikas, Timykas, and Tamecas. It doesn't matter if the name is first, second, or last. We're all invited to join Club Tamika dot com, a paid site which promises to grant us access to an international forum of Tamikas.

As I scroll down the Club Tamika page, I'm reminded that there's a Barbie doll named after us ("Singing Star Tamika"—a doll my Mom had gotten me a long time ago as a "missing you" present). I learn that Coca-Cola created a Tameka can, and that someone made a t-shirt that features a shortened version of our names ("It's a Mika Thing . . . You Wouldn't Understand"). I scroll further down the Club Tamika page. There's a YouTube video from the 43rd season of *Saturday Night Live* with a funny skit by Leslie Jones called "Get Woke With Tamika." There's even a Club Tamika book club and an annual Club Tamika cruise.

When I think about this cruise I can't help but remember the scene in *Being John Malkovich* where John Malkovich, playing himself, slides down the portal into his own person and every character in this surreal version of life looks like him, and the only word they can utter is Malkovich. But I digress.

I haven't gone on the cruise, and with further research I learn that not many other Tamikas have either. I have decided to not pay for a Club Tamika membership. I've done my own searching for fellow namesakes. I even found other Tameca Colemans, many of whom sing. One of them sang on the *Waiting to Exhale* soundtrack as part of a gospel choir. Someone asked me about that once. I remember hesitating, before confessing it wasn't me.

On Amazon I find more Tameca writers and singers. On LinkedIn, more than 400 Tamecas! Tameca is a senior analyst, realtor, human resource manager, engineer, librarian, specialist, secretary, consultant, IT tech specialist, engineer, massage therapist, photographer, nurse, bank loan specialist, esthetician, marketer, lawyer, teacher, mental health therapist, CEO, social worker, nutritionist, restaurateur, customer service agent, receptionist, nail tech, coder, security officer, retail professional, tax preparer, face melter, and health professional. Forget the cruise. We could start a whole village.

At least two other Tameca Colemans have my same middle name. At least one Tameca L Coleman is a queer photographer and writer. I tried talking with her a few of times, but it looks like she has blocked me and hid herself from Facebook search.

How to Honor Your Mother and Your Father

"I thought there was a thing called forgiveness, and if you don't want to forgive and if you don't pray for that person, it never be right."

Winter, 1976: An Interview with My Mother,
Donna Lynn Outland

I didn't want to start the day off with such bad memories
but my daughter wrote and asked me about the time
the car broke down in the south, when we were driving
From Big Spring Texas to Windsor North Carolina.

That trip was probably the worst experience in my whole life.
That's when I really saw prejudice.

I think she was six months old. Little baby in the backseat.
The car broke down in Macon County Georgia.

We were headed to see family
and to go to my husband's grandfather's funeral.

Between the police who checked on us
and the farmers who stopped for us—
They were all hateful, so unkind,
and I was afraid.

We were called all kinds of names,
all of them starting with the word nigger.

The car tire fell off and we needed gear grease to fix it.
They charged us $5 for a Coke can with a little bit of grease in it.

They kept calling my husband boy.
They kept calling him nigger.
They saw the nigger monkey baby in the back seat.
And I was the nigger lover.

We needed gas, too.
The farmers said they had some back at the farm.
I can still see my husband with the gas can in his hands.
I begged him not to go.

The Air Force sticker on the front of the car was a protective sigil.
Without it, we were nothing to these people.

I hope to never go through there again.
I'll go up over and around the south, to this day.
I've never been so afraid of white people in my life.

Once we got the car fixed, we got the hell out of there.
We made it to Windsor and we were finally
with family —

But they didn't want me there because I am white.
They glared across the driveway.

My husband's father was the only one to hug and welcome me.
The rest made me feel like an outcast.
I was only 18.

It could have been Cordova
or Denton. Preston?
Federalsburg?
Choptank?
Trappe?

I only knew we lived
on Pinetown Road
in a little yellow house
on an acre of land,
surrounded by woods and fields.

Even Pinetown Road
could have been a town
name. I always thought it was.
It was all I needed to know.

My brothers and I had a
swingset, and there was orange clay
in the backyard.

We dug it up and played chocolate
factory, formed mud and clay
into patties, pretended to eat them.

We never really did,
and we could never quite
put the mud back into the ground
the way that it was supposed to go.

Mom was mad at us for that.
There were potholes all over the yard,
patches of ripped up grass,
sunken earth.
We tried though. We really did.
I promise.

Mom loved that house. Dad helped
pay, or maybe mostly. Maybe all-paid.
His name was on the deed.

Dad, your name
was on the deed.

Mom's name was on the deed. Her blood and sweat, too.

The house was a Sweat Equity HUD
home in the country, green and bramble
surrounding, a dirt road up to the front,
two blue chicken vats
from Allen foods in the back,
and an old pull trailer
with the paint peeling off,
the thin wood
splintering.

Mom had a man come draw a panther in pencil
on the living room wall next to the front door
when Dad was at work.

It was the kind of panther you see
in those velvet paintings you get
at tourist whatnot shops in Okinawa.

Mom and Dad had one of those
in their bedroom. The man used
it as a guide.

*I remember telling your dad that whenever we moved or if we
sold that house, I was taking the wall with me but I never got
to cut that piece of wall out. I left in too much of a hurry.*

The man drew Conan the Barbarian for my two brothers' room.
It didn't quite look like him but we called him Conan, anyway.

He looked more like He-Man,
even if his windblown hair
was strapped at the temples
with a leather headband
and longer than it was in the cartoon.

I wanted something on my wall, too. I
was supposed to get Strawberry Shortcake
up there, but I didn't really like Strawberry
very much and I only had Lemon Meringue
(who rode by herself on the Strawberry
Shortcake Carousel). I didn't really play
with those toys very much. I'd set
them up in a "story," and mostly leave
them there. Barbie couldn't play,
the Cabbage Patch kid
with the two front teeth
couldn't, nor could
my brothers' Mack Truck or Hun-Dred,
the Destroyer robot. They were all toys I liked,
but they lived in different worlds.

The man suggested Care Bears then (they were on my sheets),
or anything I wanted, and I thought
maybe I'd like an owl looking over my room,
wings spread like it was flying towards me
but he never returned.

I asked Mom why.
I felt bad because
maybe I should have just said
yes to Strawberry Shortcake. Mom said she wasn't
sure why he didn't come back.
I know now why she lied.

I was told my mother was a wild woman. Dad said she was bad.
He held me close when he told me that and said everything was going to be okay.
I don't remember my father holding me like that before.

Before Mom left, he was a ghost
or mad or sitting in the living room
smoking, drinking a beer
with the TV on.

He worked and worked and worked otherwise.
One time, he even walked the long distance
when the car stopped working in the dead
cold of a blizzarding winter.

I remember Mom slowly warming his hands. Cold water
first because that's way warmer than the cold outside.

Sitting on his lap being held like that meant comfort.
He was my father then. I was not afraid, though I was confused.
His distance and anger were more prevalent in my mind.

He pointed at the broken kitchen door window and said
Mom broke it.
She got some of her things.
He had changed the locks.

Your mother is bad he said,
A bad woman. I nodded even though I wasn't sure.

She left you. She's bad.
I nodded and didn't cry.

Kids on the bus said she was a whore. I didn't know
what that word was or how'd they'd know. I didn't know what wild was
or why my Mom was bad or how she could be a whore.
That was really bad. Like ultimate bad. Mom? Kids
said stuff about you; something about fucking a man
in the convenience store freezer (they used that word—fuck;
please, don't make me chew on the soap).

In reading class, I came across the word
and started to sound it out. I looked up at the teacher,
"I can't say that word," I said. "Go ahead and sound it out,"
she said. I started crying, "I can't say that word. It's a bad
word." My friends at the table said "It's hour. It's hour."
"But there's an H," I said. The teacher encouraged "The H
is silent." She made me say the word out loud. Hour. She made me
keep reading through my tears. I'll never forget
the silent H. I'll never forget the difference.

I could never get away with anything. Mom knew everything. She always
knew when I lied, or when there was something I was trying to hide.

There was a bully on the bus who always called me names.
I was so angry at him I screamed and got sent to the principal's
office more than once.

Ms. Lynn, the principal
was tall and scary looking.
She had big shoulder pads and high heels
that made her look even meaner and taller.
There was a paddle
on her window sill. She opened the curtain up
so I could see.

The kids on the bus said she had a paddle with holes in it.
I looked for it, and didn't see it, thought that maybe it was hiding
somewhere
for special cases like me.
The kids on the bus said that kind was the worst
because it would just suck
your booty flesh through the holes.

I was trying to remember
if the principal could spank me
and whether a paddle like that was worse
than my father's snapping belt
or a fresh green switch
my parents made me break
off a nearby tree
to the house.

The kids on the bus
laughed at me when I asked.
She can't do that.
She was only trying to scare you.
You are so gullible.

The man was going to paint the pictures too, but he never came back,
so one day, Mom took our Crayolas and colored the panther,
the jungle plants and Conan, his sword and leather headband.
I remember I was upset that after she was done, the crayons
were nothing more than nubs. There were no other crayons
in the house, and she didn't want to buy new ones
because we could still use the nubs.

*He died. The cops found him in a shallow grave killed execution
style. It was really sad. He was a nice person as far as I knew.
He was a talented artist. I don't know why that happened.*

I got a bad spanking once because there was crayon scribble
on my bedroom wall. But I didn't do it. It was my baby brother. I had to
scrub
and scrub and scrub. The colors didn't want to come off the wall. I had to
use elbow grease. That's when I learned what elbow grease was.
I scrubbed and scrubbed and scrubbed. You still
think I was the one who did it, all these decades later. But
my brother was the one
who liked coloring.
I liked to tear
paper.

I remember Mom, how you joked about the next owners.
Something about how paint doesn't work very well over
wax. Too bad for them.
But I know you always wished
you could cut out the wall
and bring it with with us when we left.

[. . . insert picture of my
brothers and I
in front of mural
if Mom can find it. . . .]

I used to melt crayons in my Grandma Goldie Bell's
hot water heater. We used to live there, before the yellow house
on Pinetown Road. I got caught after only three times
because of the smell. Little kids don't know the dangers
of gas and pilot lights. I only knew
the colored wax melting was mesmerizing,
and it was like playing Operation to not get burned
or to drip wax on the little flame so that the pilot light
went out. The front room smelt like burnt wax long after that
and what the fuck was a hot water heater doing
out in the open in the living room
anyway? I remember one of my uncles
crinkling his nose. We were a house
full of people. I knew the grownups would never let it down
for at least as long as that terrible burnt crayon smell
was in the house.

The neighbor's boys—
we called them the twins—
one of them made me get into
the empty vat. He tipped it.
I was dumb. I went in.
The vat was like a cave at first
but then the boy tipped it back up
and I was too light
to tip it back down.
My brother ran inside, yelling
that he was going
to tell Mom.
The boy said he wasn't going
to let me out until
I touched it.

Mom married a man
they used to call Smiley
when she was young.

That's my Dad.
Here's a picture
of a picture
I took
when I visited
as an adult.

I didn't learn
his nickname
until that trip.

I'd gone because
my Aunt passed
and because I learned
that my father
has Parkinson's.

My father always had a lot of records,
a lot of good music, and he had that Coleman
gap in his teeth. His hair was soft and fuzzy.
He had round soft muscles. He used to write
my Mom poetry.

When I'm an adult, he'll tell me
how when Mom was pregnant with me,
he used to walk many miles to the store
to get her whatever she wanted.

Mom told me once that he was jealous I was coming

and jealous　　　　　　　when

I was there

　　　　　　　and he had even punched her

　　　　　　　　in the pregnant belly.

I must have bounced around.
The wonder and magic

and safety of the womb.

My mother's neck still shakes
from all the beatings
and rapes,

and stranglings—

even more so when
she is angry

or crying.

My mother had a hawk eye on us.
I remember when these men had come over
It was a humid summer day,
and maybe I was showing them
something.
I can't remember what.
But they were close and leaning in closer
and one of them
couldn't stop saying
how fresh I was.
"She's so fresh."
All I could think of was that song by Kool and the Gang.
"She's fresh. She's so fresh."
And I remember one of them kind of sweating a lot.
And Mom called from the doorway,
"Meca come here."
Or maybe she said something to the men.
I think she must have.
There was a feeling;
It was so strong a thing
I thought I had done something wrong.
"Don't ever
say that about my daughter again."
They had business there,
and stayed a while.
Mom made me go color
or do homework
in the kitchen.
I kept waiting for her to tell me
she was mad.

In the eighties, so many PSAs.
Some were for the children,
like how when your parents divorce,
it's not your fault. Some were
for those who would understand
that abused children
would abuse their children.
The statistics tell it.

I promised myself when I was nine
or ten, maybe even eight,
that I would never
have children of my own.

The bully on the bus always called me names. I was pretty sure I hated him. So, I wrote a note for him at school before the last bell rang and I had to get back on the bus. I tried to remember all the bad words that I couldn't hold in my mouth. You are a bitch, whore, motherfucker, you cunt ass penis sucker.

The letter was a page long; one of my only poisoned pens. I folded it up and threw it at his lap when I passed him on the bus. I watched him read it. He tore it up into little pieces. I was disappointed. I wanted him to be mad but I don't remember him bothering me after that. I don't remember him turning around. I wanted him to be mad. Maybe I even wanted to hit him in the nose. Give me a reason.

Mom ruled with a double-bind.
She taught me to walk,
one foot in front of the other.
Don't splay your feet out,
or I'll make you wear braces.
Don't slouch. Don't poke
your neck out. Stop picking
your face. Are you trying to be
ugly?

She told me to cover my body.
She told me to not let the boys
touch me or say things.

*Don't attract attention
and you'll be safe.*

Mom used to say that she was so happy I didn't get the Coleman gap tooth but it was something I always wanted. You could stick your tongue out into it. It looked funny and I tried to imagine what that would feel like. If I had a gap in my teeth I would love it and smile all the time. I wanted it as badly as I wanted red hair and freckles, like the kid from my K-3 classes did. I had a crush on him. His hair was red and straight and shiny. He sat behind me in the 3rd grade and made a joke that if we were in olden times, he'd dip the ends of my two ponytails into the inkwell. There was that one time I bent over to pick up a dropped pencil beside my desk and he didn't know I was there. He bumped into me and I could feel the softness of the front of him on my backside. I blushed and stood up very quickly. And then I let him pass.

When the bully on the bus tore the letter to shreds,
somehow, a piece of it
made its way into the driveway.
It had the word "bitch" on it
in my handwriting.
Mom found it the paper
and made me look up the word in the dictionary.
You don't even know what that word means, do you?
It's a female dog, so not so bad, shrug.
I touched the definition.
She made me eat soap anyway.

We went to Mom's and her boyfriend's every other weekend.
I know this hurt her. The law hurt her. My father hurt her.
I could see it on her face every time we came over.

On one of our weekends, she asked us if we'd like to take a trip to
Grandma and Grandpa's. We had two changes of clothes, a book to
read (my first Nancy Drew!) we got from the airport, and an activity
pad for the plane. My brothers were excited. I was angry. Does Dad
know? When are we coming back? Shouldn't we tell him?

No.

"When your mom took you guys, it hurt a lot of people."
—UNCLE JOHN. UNCLE HENRY

The twins next door,
I don't think they lived there long but they
used to come over.
I'd be doing my homework
at the kitchen table
and one of them started touching me.
Do you like that?
I could feel my shoulders brace but I didn't know why.
And if I said something I would have been in trouble.
Mom came around the corner and told them
they had to go.
She told me not to let them touch me
and that they couldn't come over anymore.
My brother used to play with them.
I think he was sad
they couldn't come over
to play.

We got a box from Maryland a long while after we'd moved. Everything inside it was doused with gasoline. I don't know how but I could feel my angry father. Our baby albums were in the box, some family photographs tossed in. Mom cried. I stole some pictures from the box. None of our toys were inside.

A friend who worked for the state pulled me aside one day and
spoke to me in a whisper. They had come across my family's file.
"It's totally illegal, but do you want his information?"
"Yes." I said. "Yes."

I was nineteen.

I fell asleep with the light
still on and woke, head
covered to deflect a bright
dissonance. A voice

from that in-between place
of sleeping and waking demanded
through gritted teeth, "Give your life."

No. I could not shake it, the whole night
could not shake it.

In dreams, he told me to make
my decision over and over. Give
me your life. I tossed and turned,
brow sweat

souring, the scrape and the burn
of a memory (No!):

My father said what matters
is blood and God. His wife
said "The daughters always return."

The next day I could not shake
it. I could not shake it.
How free I'd been.
How free.

*

I woke the next morning with my left hand on my chest,
face in the pillows.

I woke up and smiled, turned over onto my back
hand still on my chest, thankful for my life.

*

I began the next day face down in prostration.
I pushed my face into the pillows, stretched
my arms and legs as far as they would go.

Then a text from my father:
"my wife is dying",
followed by three sad face emojis.

At the bus stop, on the way to work,
someone chalked HOLY GHOST!
POWER onto the sidewalk.

I stared for twenty
minutes at what felt
like a command.

He said, my wife is dying.
He said, make your decision.
He said, curse your problems.

      I checked my account and I had
      just enough. I bought the ticket.
      I flew east. I looked into
      his eyes, and I didn't know him.
      He said he thought
      he got Parkinson's because there were
      so many things he was never able
      to say.

Your oldest sister, my aunt, has always wanted some of my poems. She doesn't know what I write. I wonder if she worries. I wonder if she would like to see because of a confluence between hope and suspicion.

The daughter who returns does so with a glad and open heart. The daughter who returns has forgiven and perhaps forgotten. She comes back home with a caring hand, and all is well in her smile.

But I am my mother's daughter and I still flinch when people touch me.

Twenty Years

My step-dad taught how to shoot hoops. I learned that if I flick my wrist
and stand square to, the ball will ease into the loop.

The year I ran long distance, he helped me control my flailing left arm.
He taught that if I hold it close to my side I can conserve my energy for
the last few hundred yards.

One afternoon I slouched over the back steps as I cried over some boy
whose name I can't remember. He told me loves break what's beating,
and I was sure to break loves too.

Then at eighteen, when I was away from his home without even a picture
to remember him by,
you came out of some mailed photographs, ghost that you were, a man in
shadows wearing colors too dark for the frame.

You and I were eight years apart then.

The pictures showed your new wife's cleanliness. Everything hung in
congruent order in a white kitchen all copper and sunned hearts.

In another photo, labeled "dad and me at a lip sing," you sheened in a vest
and chains, emulating a bare-chested Isaac Hayes. You smiled at your
Millie Jackson as she sang to you her silent part of the duet.

I saw children peeking from between your legs. This was not the
workaholic father I never saw when I was ten, who my mother left then
because of welting anger and flying hands.

I stuffed the pictures into some deep odd box, until twelve more years
apart allowed me to pick up the phone when I had landed near you.

Will you come see me?

You drove five hours, paid for the overpriced hotel room.

You knew we didn't have much time before I had to take a flight back home.

In our moments, we said little. You comfortably drifted to sleep, while I waited. The TV blasted some rerun show or the news. And then, the time was gone.

I could not understand how small you were, how soft. I could not decipher recognition from the contours of your face.

I gave you five of the disheveled poems from the bottom of my bag. You were so thankful, for crumpled stains and scribbles over typewritten text.

The poems were discards. I hadn't even signed my name, and I wouldn't call you again for a long time after that.

After My Father's Wife Died

"I'm sorry that you can't make it but that's why I always depend on the Lord to help me out with my problems so probably when you decide to come see me I'll be in a casket dead. I'm sorry to say it this way but that's the way I feel. I knew this was going to happen. You had to make a decision on what you want to do. So you made your decision and I had to make my decision on different things too. So don't get disappointed on my decisions.

"Thank you. Thank you very much for being my daughter. That's the only thing I am thankful for. My sons don't want to come see me. They don't know me. This happened and that happened. I thought there was a thing called forgiveness, and if you don't want to forgive nobody for what happened, and if you don't pray for that person, you never be, it never be right.

"Instead of just living and thinking about the past—I don't think about the past. I think about the future.

"So, I'm signing out. I gotta get prepared, see my wife at the funeral home, see how she looks. Maybe I will talk with you later. Bye."

Uncle John

My Mom says none of you know how bad it was.

We were afraid of him.

You say, the only thing we have now is what's ahead, we can only move forward. I nod and decide I'm going to try that out. I say, "Let's pick him up and go to Rehoboth Beach." Everyone thinks that's a fine idea. You, Aunt Barbara, my two cousins, my father, and me. We all go.

It's off season and the weather is a bit chilly. We go to Aunt Barbara's favorite place for french fries and somebody gets some sweet and salty popcorn. Most of the shops are closed, though, and there aren't many people walking the plaza.

When I was little, my bare feet scrunched the sand. I cried when the tide took my bucket out into the waves. But then, we were about to leave, the waves brought the bucket back to me. I remember the elation.

My father was always a good dresser. When we all visited the beach, he wore a crisp baseball cap and chinos that looked like they were just off the rack. He wore a stylish bright red sweater and shoes that looked brand new.

His face was smiling but frozen, the Parkinson's already doing its work. I could see that he was happy to see me but I didn't know what to feel. I looked back towards the beach. It was windy, and cold and vacant.

[...coal and kindling....]

[This little light is memory,
a composite of many days made one.]

In a sweltering church where music so big
and bright it could ignite this room,
blow everything open
from the bench splinters out

[This little light is a hymnal page
turning.]

voices rise up;
the house band keeps time;
the pastor stirs up the congregation.

Benches begin to rock and tremble
like the quaking of God might —
women fly out their seats shouting Hallelujah
Amen Praise Him Oh Jesus Sweet Jesus Praise Him
and god! Their tongues twisting

joy and sorrow, babble
as their bodies writhe
out of time in the music.

> [This little light is a shout
> Hallelujah! Amen.]

They speak into the air, their eyes
wild as they sift into god.

They are raptured, holy,
swept into their most private ecstasies.
The benches tremble. The floor thumps.
The congregation knows the song.

> [This little light
> is tongue speaking women.]

I want to hold that power.

> [This little light is sinners
> come to be reborn.]

I hold
the book, stare at the words
and the dots and lines,
listen to the song but I cannot sing.
I listen to the song,
yearn to fly up
or burst open.

> [This little light warms as the hymnal pages turn,
> dots and lines along the page:
> coal and kindling.]

Big brown curvy angels—their hands,
their husbands' hands, their lovers, their children,
clap more rhythm into the driving beat. They clap
more rhythm and I cannot move from this seat. They clap more rhythm,
amplifying tension, sound, vibration, the heat in these packed pews.
Their throats, upturned, fill the room.

> [This little light
> is a prickling in my skin.]

The whole building is shaking now—this god's house —
this beautiful turbulence, veritable hells
being sweated out of their temples
and out of every crevice God gave them.

> [This little light
> is sudden devotion.]

I turn to see my father beside me.
It is the first memory I have of him.
And I am confused seeing him like this:

> [This little light
> is a cleansing fire. Amen.]

A strain marks his face,
his hat is in his lap, crushed by his fidgeting fingers;
his body rocks and sweat pools, drips
a waterline from his temples to his collarbones,
separating himself from who he was
and who is becoming.

> [This little light
> is my father beside me.]

He is no longer an angry ghost of flying hands.
"God wants me back," he says. "God
wants me back."

100

[...testify....]

I only know I love him because of this memory:
I was witness to my father in the turn.

He'd been a ghost til then, hardened by military muscle
and work and cigarette smoke, a history marked
by his own father's flying hands,
the same man who brought my brothers and I sweets and coins,
the same who took us crabbing and taught us
how to crack a crab leg and that the mustard tasted good.

Grandpa was soft while sober and when drunk,
wrathful as the Old Testament.

    *

It was in that moment I saw him, no longer fuzzy
like the face from a dream that evaporates with sunlight.

I could see we had the same nose, the same
tendency for a dry and cracking lower lip.

He was soft like a child,
the ailing parts of his life beading
across his face, raining from his head.

There was a tension in his face like he was crying
or shitting.

* notes

They asked me whose daughter/ I was. I do not know whose/ daughter I am.

"Santeria teaches that, just as everyone has an earthly mother and father, each person also has an orisha mother and father." From: *Cuban Santeria: Walking with the Night* by Raul Canizares. p. 54.

———————

"Inside, Outside, The Ocean." This poem was written fairly quickly after my first time reading through Édouard Glissant's book *Poetics of Relation*, and it is especially influenced by the section entitled "The Open Boat."

———————

. . . wish you knew how it would feel to be free.
Like a bird in the sky. How sweet that would be!

This is a loose quote from "I Wish I Knew How It Would Feel To Be Free" as performed by Nina Simone on the album Silk & Soul, 1967. Written by Billy Taylor and Richard Carroll Lamb (Dick Dallas).

"High yellow girl, can't you tell / you're just the surface of our dark deep well? / If your mind could really see / you'd know your color the same as me."

Hearing these lines for the first time stopped me in my tracks and split my heart. The lyrics are from "We Are the People Darker Than Blue", as performed by Curtis Mayfield on the album *Curtis*. Found via Spotify, originally recorded at RCA Studios in Chicago, 1970.

———————

"Now people choose their identities. Now people choose to be Black. They used to be *born* Black. That's not true anymore. You can be Black genetically and choose not to be. You can change your mind or your eyes, change anything. It's just a mindset." From *Conversations with Toni Morrison*, edited by Danille Taylor-Guthrie. (New York: University of Mississippi Press, 1994), p. 236. This idea is reiterated through one of Morrison's characters in her book *Tar Baby*.

———————

Ourika

"About this time talk started of emancipating the Negroes. Of course, this question passionately interested me. I still cherished the illusion that at least somewhere else in the world there were others like myself. I knew they were not happy and I supposed them noble-hearted. I was eager to know what would happen to them. But alas, I soon learned my lesson. The Santo Domingo massacres gave me cause for fresh and heartrending sadness. Till then I had regretted belonging to a race of outcasts. Now I had the same of belonging to a race of barbarous murderers." From *Ourika* by Claire de Duras, translated by John Fowles (New York: The MLA Association of America, 1994), p.21.

———————

"That moment in *Black-ish* when Dre tells Bow she's not really Black." *Black-ish*, "Pilot", Hulu, directed by James Griffiths (2014; ABC)

———————

"Jean Toomer." *Poetry Foundation*, Poetry Foundation, www.poetryfoundation.org/poets/jean-toomer. Accessed April 2018.

James Brown's "Say It Loud, I'm Black & I'm Proud," is a single originally released in 1968.

"That moment when Rebecca Walker warns that "if we remain mesmerized by the idea of ourselves as eternally broken, we all but guarantee the loss of our lives as fully functional, whole human beings." Prasad, Chandra. *Mixed: An Anthology of Short Fiction on the Multiracial Experience*. W.W. Norton & Co., 2006. From the introduction written by Rebecca Walker, p. 17.

For all practical purposes, 'race' is not so much a biological phenomenon as a social myth" is from *Four Statements on the Race Question*. 1969, p. 33, *Four Statements on the Race Question*. unesdoc.unesco.org/images/0012/001229/122962eo.pdf.

"When you call yourself an Indian or a Muslim or a Christian or a European, or anything else, you are being violent" is from J. Krishnamurti's *Freedom from the Known*. HarperOne, an Imprint of HarperCollins Publishers, 1969. p. 51-52.

"B-L-A-C-K, N-U-S-S. B-L-A-C-K, N-U-S-S. B-L-A-C-K, N-U-S-S. B-L-A-C-K, Black is okay!" From Rahsaan Roland Kirk's song "Blacknuss", from the album *Blacknuss* (Atlantic Records, 1971).

* images [index of captions]

* acknowledgements

Ultimately this work is my work but I would be remiss if I did not acknowledge the many teachers, mentors, guides, and peers who read, edited, encouraged, suggested readings, and advised I send my manuscript to the wonderful editors at The Elephants. If I have forgotten anyone in this note of thanks, please know that my forgetfulness is not deliberate.

The bulk of this manuscript came together during my time at the Mile-High MFA at Regis University. Guidance from the following mentors often changed the course of the work, giving it focus, depth, and also allowed freedom to try out hybridities and to "trust the catalogue" when I was unable to write it straight. Thank you Kathy Fish, Jenny Shank, Lori Ostlund, Khadijah Queen, Eric Baus, and Andrea Rexilius for giving so much that I still carry with me, and so much more that continues to be points of study going forward. Big thanks to peers who workshopped pieces of this manuscript during our MFA residencies, and much gratitude to David Hicks and Martin McGovern for starting the program where I met all of these wonderful people and more.

I am beyond thankful to the writers who read all or part of this work, including Steven Dunn, Thuyanh Astbury, Suzi Q. Smith, E.A. Midnight, Hillary Leftwich, Arielle Lyric, Ahja Fox, D.L. Cordero, Alexandra

Jackson, Brian Lupo, Maha Kamal, and Joe Ponce. Your eyes on this work have helped me to see so much, and I have learned from all of your work, as well. I have so much admiration for every single one of you.

Some of the poems in this book were first drafted during my undergraduate degree at then named Metropolitan State College of Denver under the tutelage of poets Renee Ruderman and Dr. Sandra Maresh Doe. I would also like to thank Dr. Tat Sang So for so much about discussions in craft that have become foundational in my writing.

I am thankful for literary angels who move through our communities without the need for acknowledgement, and who I sometimes earnestly reach out to in thanks. There have been so many times when I felt like giving up, and one or more of you have reached out for no reason showing me there's worth in something I am doing. I hope that I can reciprocate your warmth and gifts. You all are part of the community that has grown me, and I hope to always remember this.

I need to thank Selah Saterstrom for a tarot reading whose message led me to add the first poem in this book to this manuscript.

During my MFA, I began sessions with an incredible therapist as a way to not only work towards healing of traumas, but to find the understanding and words I needed to begin to work towards reconciliation which is something I yearn for greatly. In therapy, I also learned about what was mine, and what wasn't, and I was given tools to be able to do this work and any work going forward. These tools are invaluable and have saved me. They have helped me to begin steps towards reconciliation, and I hope movement towards restoration if it is too late. I feel that final piece is not my work alone.

* bio

Tameca L Coleman is a singer, multi-genre writer, itinerant nerd and point and shoot art dabbler in Denver Colorado. Their work explores heartbreak and healing, finding the words for our experiences, familial estrangement, being 'in-between' things, finding beauty, even during times of strife, and movement towards reconciliation. Their writings have been published in *pulpmouth*, *Rigorous Magazine*, *Inverted Syntax*, *Full Stop Reviews*, *Heavy Feather Review*, *Lambda Literary*, and more. Their photography has been featured in literary magazines and in other venues. For more information about Tameca's work, follow them on social media at @sireneatspoetry.